I0480276

The Secrets To Selling Your Art Online

CATAPULT YOUR SALES IN 30 DAYS

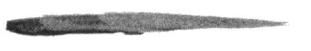

by Lucia Livingston

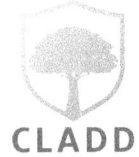

CLADD

Copyright © 2017 by Cladd Publishing Inc.
All rights reserved.

Except as permitted under the United States Copyright act of
1976, no part of this publication may be reproduced or
distributed in any form or by any means, or stored in a
database or retrieval system, without prior written permission
of the publisher.

Cladd Publishing Inc.
USA

This publication is designed to provide accurate information
regarding the subject matter covered. It is sold with the
understanding that neither the author nor the publisher is
providing medical, legal or other professional advice or
services. Always seek advice from a competent professional
before using any of the information in this book. The author
and the publisher specifically disclaim any liability that is
incurred from the use or application of the contents of this
book.

The Secrets To Selling Your Art Online: Catapult Your Sales In
30 Days

ISBN 978-1-946881-08-3 (e-book)
ISBN 978-1-946881-07-6 (paperback)

Contents

Chapter 1: Where Do I Start?

When you're ready to sell your art, what's the best way to start? Who do you contact; and where do you go?

1. One market is made up of art collectors
2. The other is just regular, everyday people
3. Licensing to companies and organizations

If you're serious about selling your art, it's vital to figure out which group you're going to target *BEFORE* you begin.

Let's say you want to sell your artwork to fine art connoisseurs. Great! You'll probably want to be represented by a gallery. If not, you will need to put all your fears aside and prepare for a whole new world of self-promotion.

Chapter 2: Finding Your Perfect Buyer

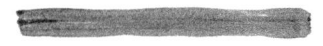

Many artists sell work themselves out of their studio, online, at co-operative galleries, or even at one of the thousands of art fairs across the nation. However, just because you are an artist doesn't mean that you know how to sell your work. In fact, most artists desperately struggle with the sales and marketing aspect of their business.

4 WAYS TO FIND YOUR PERFECT BUYER

1. **How do you sell your art?**
   The most common response is "I don't sell my art." If you can respond to this with a different answer then you are ahead of the pack already.

2. **Who is your ideal audience?**
   Most artists don't give this question nearly as much consideration as they should, which is a shame because the answer to this question is key to success. You will need to know who buys the art you are creating, for you to hone in on that particular audience. Without this target audience, you will spin your wheels and never

move an inch. Or waste your money throwing ads at the wrong group of people.

3. **What kind of art do you make?**
   Can you speak about your work? Is your artist's statement interesting? Or is it dull and confusing with redundancy?

   Be ready to talk about your work, and share your passion. Tell a story, take them on a journey and explain the intricate details that make the creation special to you. Understand that not everyone can be inside your head. And more often than you would imagine, people are intimidated by art, they fear looking stupid.

   Educating people about your work, making them feel comfortable to engage in a conversation with you, will go a long way toward building a lifelong clientele.

4. **Where will your work find its audience?**
   Always be ready to sell your art. Have a business card on you always, make sure your website, phone, email, gallery, or social media page is clearly listed.

Have your work documented with all of your professional materials ready to go at a moment's notice. Opportunity does not wait for you to get your act together. As a professional artist, you never know when you might meet someone who could open a door for you. Prepare for your success. Because when could be now.

Chapter 3: Building Instant Value: Create A Maker's Story

Telling your story, building character and purpose
for your piece

It's a wonderful time to be an artist. It is now possible to share your work with customers from around the world, all without leaving the comfort of your studio.

But with this abundance of opportunity comes an increase in competition. For many makers, this global audience brings up a tricky question: In a sea of creative artist, how do you stand out? *By sharing your unique story of course.*

By focusing on these three elements, you'll create an authentic maker's story that builds your personality and increases the value of your work. The result is a story that showcases your authentic vision and builds a tremendous amount of loyalty from your customers.

3 SIMPLE WAYS TO CREATE A PROFITABLE MAKER'S STORY

1. **Your Background**
   Walk your visitors through your artistic journey, showing who you are, and what inspired your creation. Sharing these details in a genuine, authentic way will help customers feel more connected to you and your work. Buyers need a story to share with their friends and family, so give them one they can enjoy telling for years to come.

2. **Your Inspiration**
   Sharing your inspiration tells the philosophy behind your work and the incredible amount of thought and care that went into each creation.

3. **Your Process**
   This is the perfect place to get creative, sharing a peek inside your sketchbook or a snapshot of in-progress pieces.

   While these things may seem commonplace to you, not everyone is an artist. What you do is downright magical to your buyers and they mystified at behind the scenes look at your creative process. Demonstrating your expertise proves just how much time you've invested in your craft, giving customers a new appreciation

for your skill and increasing the perceived
value of your work.

Chapter 4: Signature Styles & Banking on Your Weakness

If you look at the work of any of the top artists in the world, you will notice that each has a recognizable style. It might be the subjects they paint, the artistic style, their palette, or any combination of things that makes their work recognizable. This recognition adds importance and value to the art, as collectors want art that is reflective of an artist's body of work, and galleries prefer to exhibit a range of diverse artists, rather than a diverse range by one artist.

Using your weakness to create a strong style, is one of the most profound ways to change an artist from average to exceptional. What you have been hiding from your whole life is what you now need to make yourself stand out from the rest.

Weakness = Interesting Art = Increased Value

For example: Marian thinks she is horrible at making clouds in the sky. She believes they look like cotton candy gone wrong. Thus, for years she has been avoiding scenery paintings that would require her to paint clouds. As here coach I had Marian complete a sky scene so that I could see what all the fuss was about. I had her repeat the same painting on a separate canvas, but this time I painted the clouds in a way she enjoyed.

Now that I have two paintings, one with her cotton candy clouds, and one with my realistic looking clouds; we took the paintings down to her local market. We asked each passer buyer to tell us which painting they liked the best.

Over 80% enjoyed her cotton candy gone wrong clouds, because it was unique and interesting. We also asked them to tell us what each painting was worth, and 96% rated the cotton candy cloud painting as being more valuable, regardless of which one they preferred hanging on their wall at home.

Being Original Means Embracing Your Strengths & Weaknesses

What makes a great artist is when they embrace both their strengths and weakness into one form. If you cannot make a hand for anything, then what you ended up with will look as though you meant it appear unique from the other work. The weakness becomes your signature touch that separates you from the sea of other artists.

❖ Do not be afraid to be unique, life's true beauty comes from its imperfections.

Chapter 5: Developing a Niche

How can I establish myself to become well known and recognized for a very specific kind of art (niche)? There is only one way to be considered an expert in a certain niche, do it well, do it for a long time, and do lots of it.

Now some of you will already have a particular type of niche you enjoy, and have been doing for a while. However, many of you are still deciding what niche, if any, you would like to dedicate your life to. There are many benefits to becoming known in a certain field. Therefore, it is important that you really ask yourselves the following questions to determine what is right for you.

HOW TO FIND YOUR NICHE

- Focus on interest that you feel passionate about.
- If you love what you're doing, you'll stay dedicated long enough to see success. You'll also do your best work.
- The power of the niche is the old "big fish in a little pond" idea. There is a higher probability

that you will become well known for something when you focus on one small area.

BECOME KNOWN FOR YOUR STYLE

- Be that artist with that unmistakable style.
- You don't have to see their name on the work to know they did it.

BECOME KNOWN AS A LOCAL ARTIST (AT LEAST GEOGRAPHICALLY)

- Become known as "the artist of your town" and over time, you will be the first person that comes to mind for local projects.

BECOME KNOWN FOR A LIFESTYLE

- Take what you love; a hobby, a passion, and charity; and mend that with your talent to create a niche.

STILL NEED HELP FINDING YOUR NICHE? REFLECT ON WHAT YOU HAVE DONE

Ask yourself the following questions to gain additional clarity:
- What do I love doing the most?

- Which of my works of art makes me the proudest?
- What do I really feel passionate about?

REFLECT ON WHAT YOU HAVE DONE

- What project did I do in the past that I really enjoyed?
- Why was it so easy for me? Was it the people, the medium, the project, or something else?

AND ASK YOURSELF THIS FINAL QUESTION

- Where do I WANT to focus my time and efforts if money was no object?

Be kind to yourself, and allow plenty of time for all of this to sink in. Often, the answers are right there and we don't realize it.

Chapter 6: Using Currents Trends to Maximize Sales

Getting in the trend can be a powerful tool to help new and experienced artist sale more pieces. Find something that everyone is crazy about and start there. If elephants are the thing, then start by creating the animal with your own unique spin.

Every artist needs a special style that carries throughout their piece. It is your personality coming through into your work and separates your art from others. Buyers rarely remember art with no personality or uniqueness.

The idea of using current trends is to catapult your work into the mainstream. Since these trends are being searched regularly, you will have a higher chance of being found. As the trends change and morph into other interest, so will your art. It is a fun and easy way of finding inspiration that people are currently looking to purchase.

Chapter 7: Gallery Representation

Getting a gallery to show your work can be tough for new artists, but it's not impossible. One thing that will help is to have an entire series of work ready to show, based around a specific idea.

The reason why this will work is because the show can be made up of just your artwork, and that makes it easy on gallery managers to plan the event and appeal to a niche market.

Once you've got a series ready, then call your local galleries and set up appointments to speak with them about your art. Have an artist statement and resume ready for your meeting.

Keep in mind that many galleries plan shows a year in advance. Which means even if you do get accepted, your work may not be shown right away. While you're waiting, keep creating and try to line up more shows, so you can stay busy throughout the year.

❖ But perhaps you're like many artist and would rather not split your earnings with a gallery.

Chapter 8: Dealer Galleries - Why the High Commission?

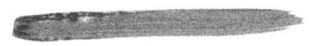

Galleries typically charge a 50% commission on the sale of two-dimensional artwork.

- Paintings
- Photos,
- Monotypes

They charge up to 40% for three-dimensional work. For an artist who is not currently making much money, it's difficult to imagine how it could make sense to work with a gallery. What could a gallery do that would possibly be worth the commission of 30-50%?

The truth is, that it doesn't makes sense for every artist. But for some of you, it could be exactly what you were looking for.

WHY WOULD I PAY COMMISSION?

Let's say you have a painting, sculpture or photograph that you have priced at $1,000. If you sell the art yourself, you'll get the full $1,000. If a gallery sells it you will make $500-$600.

If that was all the math that you had to do, this would be a slam dunk. Of course, you would rather take the $1,000 over $500. But to come to the real value of a gallery, we need to dive a little deeper.

THE VALUE OF ART CONSIST OF TWO THINGS

1. One part of the value is created by your talents and creativity to produce the work.
2. The second part is created by all of the time, effort, and cost that goes into marketing, promoting, and selling.

Which is more difficult, creating the art or selling it? Every artist would have a different answer to this question, but I suspect that a majority of artists feel it's much easier to create art than it is to sell it. When you sell your own art, you've done all of the work and you earn the full $1,000 value. If a gallery has sold the work for you, you have hired them to take over the marketing, sales, and customer service for you.

Now, all you have to do is figure out how much value you can create per hour in the studio, vs. how long it takes you to sell a piece of art yourself. If you generate more value in the studio than selling, you should be working toward finding galleries to take over the sales for you.

Many times, the gallery can sell your art for much more than what you could. Buy riding on the shoulders of their reputation and elegant display setting, you may end up making more money and doing less work!

I have met many artists over the years who are born salespeople as well as great artists. If you, like sales, find it easy, fun, and exciting, then paying for gallery representation is not worth it.

Chapter 9: Selling Art Directly to The Public

Selling to the public means you have access to a much larger audience, and the easiest way to tap into that is by choosing a certain group of people and creating work just for them. After all, the average person is much more inclined to buy art that speaks to their interests than anything else.

The possibilities are endless. You could create your art using sports cars; animals, boats, trees, fields, airplanes, world maps. Each of those topics are "targeted" to a specific consumer. Whatever subject you choose is fine, although it is best to have some interest in it yourself.

- *Here's an example:* Let's say you love birds, so that's what you decide to work with. Once you've created two or three pieces, you will need to find places were people interested in birds gather.
- Look for bird associations, bird watching tours, online groups and magazines. Make a list of all the possible places that might want to either buy your art, or display it to their customers.

No matter what you create, this process will work since they are pre-qualified buyers.
- With all the online forums and groups available today, it is easy to find a large audience of like-minded individuals that would love to purchase your art.

Chapter 10: Turning Buyers into Collectors

As an artist, it seems like you're pouring your heart and soul into the works you create. That's why it's so wonderful when someone falls in love with your art and decides to purchase.

Just knowing that you've somehow connected with a stranger who was able to see the beauty and value in what you've created is such a fulfilling moment. What many artists don't realize, is that a sale isn't the end game. The artist can and should use the opportunity of selling an artwork to turn a one-time buyer into a long-term collector.

It's easy to see such a purchase as the final element of the story. However, in order for you to turn a onetime buyer into a collector, you must consider a sale to be a marketing opportunity.

A CUSTOMER IS THE BEST "LEAD" YOU CAN ASK FOR

- They already like your style of work.
- You know they are a buyer of art.

Use the initial purchase to learn more about their needs.

The process that leads up to their first purchase of your art is wonderful, but it also allows you to learn more about their specific needs.

- What are their motivations?
- Their tastes?
- Where are they going to be displaying your piece?
- Do they have other needs for artwork?
- Do they purchase art regularly?
- What made them interested in buying yours?
- Why did your art appeal to them?

All this information can be useful later. In addition, by appearing interested, you will also engage the buyer, making them feel valued.

PERSONALIZING YOUR SALES PITCH: USE THE INFORMATION TO ADDRESS THEIR NEEDS

By asking the Questions listed above, you are flawlessly personalizing your sales pitch/marketing strategy to that future collector. By discussing these elements with the person who is buying your art, you'll be able to create a custom marketing plan to encourage that buyer to repurchase for years to come.

The best way to encourage a second purchase from a buyer is to make sure they don't forget you.

- Follow up with them. You don't have to call them at home (in fact, it may be too personal), but it is easy to stay in touch in this digital age.
- Encourage them to sign up for your mailing list, follow your blog, or become a fan of your professional social media page.
- Your art buyers are people who have already proven that they love your work, so who better to keep in touch with.
- Make a calendar on your computer that has your buyers' birthdays. On their birthday, you can send a personalized greeting with one of your new works,

- Create spreadsheets/lists based on interests. That way, you can have a newsletter specific to your buyers known likes.
- Keep a file on your art buyer. Simply make a page that has the name of the artwork they purchased, their name, names of loved ones they mentioned, contact information, upcoming needs or projects, birthday, and any special details you remember from your conversation. Review these files every now and then, and you can follow up with each buyer when you have something relevant to update them with. These little touches can be surprisingly effective, multiplying that connection they once felt to you and your work. They'll recognize that you're putting effort into maintaining a relationship, and it will remind them of what originally inspired them to buy your art.

FOLLOWING UP

You will want to focus energy on your social media pages and e-mail updates/newsletters. Be sensible about how often you are updating your pages and how frequently you send updates to your buyers. There's a line between 'staying in touch' and be annoying. The frequency of your updates depends on the method of communication:

- Email updates can be sent approximately once a month (maybe twice, if there is a very special update).
- You can update your social media several times a week, with shorter messages and content.
- Concentrate your updates at times of year when you know people are looking to purchase art (like the holiday season).
- You can also offer gift vouchers, for those who may want to give your work as a gift but don't feel comfortable picking it out for someone else.
- Some popular social media updates can include "behind the scenes" videos, photographed or written updates.
- You can use your social media or email updates to offer special deals or competitions. You could offer a print of your work as a prize for, or allow your fans to vote on which image you should use for your holiday greetings cards. Keep it fun and light.

The visual aspect of your communications is as important as the content. You're an artist, so you want it to look appealing and eye-catching. Do not be drab, use your signature style to make everything you do stand out.

- ✓ A shopping cart icon is the best way to let people know when a work is available for sale.
- ✓ Make sure that your site is user friendly.
- ✓ Make sure that a buyer can easily find, click and purchase your items.
- ✓ Always make it easy to find your contact information.
- ✓ Make the buying experience wonderful from start to finish.

You do not want to be that artist who is putting an extreme amount of effort into marketing and sales-generating, and then no one can easily purchase your work? It sounds obvious, but this is a critical mistake that many artists are regularly making.

DON'T BE HARD TO FIND

- Maintain an updated online presence through your website, blog, or social media channels.
- Include important details on your business cards and other promotional material.
- If you change your e-mail address, phone number, or physical address, update your materials and announce it to your followers.

Whether you're selling online or at your physical location, simplify the purchase process. The vast majority of sales are abandoned at checkout, due to difficulties making the purchase.

- If you have your own website, invest in a web developer who can make the check-out process easy and secure.
- Your online gallery should have clear images that appeal to the buyer, and they must be easy to navigate and enlarge.
- If you're showing in a gallery, make sure they are open during reasonable hours and have someone available to answer questions to prospective buyers.

Future buyers and previous purchasers will be interested in where you're showing next, and what new works you're displaying. It's good marketing to make sure that people know you're an active member of the art community. It's also a great opportunity to encourage people to come down and see what new piece you have been working on.

❖ Hold open studio days once a month, or let people know when you'll be in the gallery in person.

Chapter 11: Designing A Buyer Friendly Website

If you are an artist and you don't have a website at this current time, or if you want to change the one you have now, it's never too late! The benefits of having a website are obvious. Potential buyers looking for art can find you by Googling your name or your type of artwork, and they can contact you to make purchases.

EVERY SITE WILL BE DIFFERENT, BUT THE BASICS ARE THE SAME

- Easy-to-find contact information.
- A short bio, artist's statement.
- Images of your artwork.
- A maker's story for each piece.
- Excellence images of your art with a zoom function.
- User friendly site.
- Easy checkout and pay.

Website Building Options

WordPress.com

WordPress is well-known as a blogging platform, but it is commonly used to build a regular website using static pages. It's likely the most customizable option short of a custom-built site, with hundreds of different themes, and many options for beautiful galleries and slideshows of your work.

Keep in mind that WordPress is an excellent site if you plan on creating a blog to enhance the sale of your work.

Heavybubble.com

Unlike WordPress, Heavy Bubble is designed specifically for artists, with easy-to-set up templates for galleries, artist bios, links, and contact form.

OtherPeoplesPixels.com

This is a great option geared toward artists. Other People's Pixels promises "the best shameless-self-promotion that money can buy."

Fine Art Studio Online Faso.com

FASO includes easy to use image collections, events, and built-in visitor statistics. Two features that may make it more attractive are the option to sell artwork through the website, and a way to manage and send newsletters.

Decisions, decisions

There are lots of other things to consider than price alone.

- ✓ How is the technical support?
- ✓ Do you have the ability to create the site using their available tools?
- ✓ Can you track visitors?
- ✓ Are image galleries attractive and easy to, post and manage?
- ✓ Do they have an easy way to set up a mobile site so it looks good on smartphones?

Chapter 12: Pros & Cons of Printing & Shipping Options

Print & Ship Yourself Method

If you print them yourself, you will need to buy a color printer if you don't already have one.

PROS:

- More profits per print.
- You can easily offer signed, special and limited editions.
- You can adapt to issues more quickly.
- Mailing them out yourself can be a fantastic way to give the package your own special touch.

CONS:

- You need to buy a printer, ink and paper.
- You need to produce high quality prints.
- Handle the packaging and shipping cost/labor.
- Handle returns and damaged packages.
- Eat the cost of mistakes.

Print & Ship on Demand Method

Upload your images to a Print on Demand service, which will host a shop for you. People buy the prints, and the company prints & sends them out directly to the buyer.

PROS:

- You don't suffer cost of print mistakes.
- You do not have to print.
- You do not have to handle shipping or packaging labor/cost.
- You do not have to receive returns.
- You do not have to purchase printers, ink, labels, packaging, paper.
- You do not need extra space in your home or studio for supplies.
- You will have more time to work on your art.

CONS:

- You don't get as much profit per piece.
- Some companies only pay out when your sales reach a certain level like $25-100.
- The packaging will feel more commercial.

Chapter 13: Digital Prints & Giclees

A giclee is also known as an inkjet or digital print which offers artists a plethora of new ways to make and sell art at reasonable prices.

Even though the term giclee, digital print, and inkjet print all mean the same thing and can be used interchangeable. Artists, publishers and galleries currently represent digital art in so many different ways that unless you know your terminology, printing processes and what questions to ask, figuring out what you're looking at can often be confusing.

And when potential buyers get confused, they tend to refrain from buying. Or when they do buy and get something other than what they thought, you will have a problem on your hands. So being clear and direct about what you're selling, and how it's priced, is an important part of making the digital print selling process work smoothly.

1. **Original digital works of art.** Images conceived and created entirely on a computer that exist only as digital files until they're printed out.
2. **Original digital photographs.** Photographs that are taken with a camera and printed out directly from the original digital files or original negatives.
3. **Digital reproductions or copies of original works of art**. Images of existing works of art like paintings, photographs, watercolors, screen prints, etc. that are either photographed or scanned or uploaded into a computer, and then printed out to look the same as the originals.

Digital art of all types is rapidly increasing in popularity, regardless of whether the finished products are reproductions, originals, or some combination of the two. Whatever you want to make is fine because as with all art, there are no rules governing what artists can or cannot do.

Most giclee prints are reproductions or copies of pre-existing works of art in other mediums (like paintings, watercolors or drawings) that are either photographed or scanned into computers and then printed out to look exactly the same as the originals.

Producing giclee limited edition reproduction prints is a great way for artists to make images of their art more widely available at lower prices. This also increases their collector base by offering affordable alternatives to more expensive originals. If someone loves a particular image, and the only way they can own it is by buying it in the form of a signed limited inkjet print, that's perfectly OK. You can also sell your images as unsigned unlimited editions at even lower prices if you want to make them more affordable yet.

ARTISTS CAN SIGN, OR LIMIT, DIGITAL IMAGES OF THEIR ART IN A VARIETY OF WAYS

- Options include signing
- Numbering
- Dating
- Adding small original drawings in the margins
- Highlighting them with brush strokes of acrylic or watercolor
- Or whatever else you want to do to personalize or individualize your digital images, make them more attractive to buyers, as well as allow you to price them higher than those without any of these extras.

The options or variations you offer and how much you decide to charge for them are entirely up to you.

- Set edition sizes in advance.
- Make them public.
- Never change size and exclusivity of the edition.

In other words, if you state up front that a print is being published in an edition of twenty, keep it that way no matter how much people love it, or how fast it sells out. If you sell out a limited edition print and then decide to print more because it sold so well, you can be sure the people who bought the first printing will never buy from you again.

Selling out an edition is always good for your career and reputation. To begin with, it shows future buyers that your work is in demand. It's also an incentive for people to buy faster the next time you release a print rather than risk missing the opportunity if it sells out again. The best part about sold-out editions is that they can sometimes increase in value and sell for more than the original issue prices on resale markets. This is a sign you can begin to increase your prices on future work.

Include a detailed <u>original</u> invoice or certificate of authenticity with each image:

- Print's title.
- Paper type.
- Printer type.
- Ink type.
- Date printed.
- Edition size, or other particulars.
- Then personally sign and date it.

Not only do buyers appreciate the extras, but good documentation also tends to increase a work of art's value. Smart buyers will choose the one with documentation over the one without 100% of the time.

Artist who create original digital compositions entirely on a computer, should follow the same procedures as artists printing reproductions of works in other mediums.

For those of you who plan on producing lots of inkjet prints, think seriously about buying your own equipment rather than hiring fine art printers to do the job, or perhaps buying equipment together with several other artists. Printer prices have fell in recent years to the point where they can pay for themselves in a short period of time.

As equipment becomes more affordable, outsourcing printers is becoming less cost-effective. However, if you are specializing in high-end art, you may want to use a printing company known for producing top quality work.

ADDITIONAL TIPS

- Shop around and compare prices between printing companies.
- Get references from other artists.
- Make sure your image files are large enough to produce superior quality prints.
- Use printers capable of printing in high resolution.
- Color fields should be crisp and clean with no overlap or fuzzy edges.

KNOW THE CHARACTERISTICS OF YOUR INKS

- Under what conditions will they fade?

- Are they water-resistant?
- Should they be protected with finishes?
- Should they be displayed only in low light?

If you want your art to last, use the best ink, paper, and protective coatings available.

Experiment with different papers or other substrates to see what makes your images look the best, as well as with different surface textures and finishes. Use pigmented inks only, and get information about how long they last. Check what's referred to as their "fade characteristics". Certain inks fade substantially over time.

Chapter 14: Developing An Online Presence

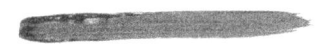

Selling Art on Instagram

HOW TO SELL ART ON INSTAGRAM

- Make great art and be consistent.
- Complete your profile to the fullest extent.
- Post images that are professional and properly lit.
- Learn how to use hashtags.
- Include many details about your artwork and where to get more.
- Identify people who are influential.
- Identify possible clients, where they hangout and who influences them.
- Track your progress.
- Try some fan-generated fun. Instagram can be great for contests, and giveaways.

Create A Fan Base & Sell Art On Facebook

7 WAYS TO TURN FACEBOOK INTO A MONEY MACHINE

It is most important to develop a reputation with your collectors/fanbase before you can really start selling your art. Engage with potential buyers and build interest through your work.

- Post photos of your work during development.
- Post an artwork from your past, childhood, present. Show where you've come from.
- Start an interesting topic: talk about your process, what you're working on, what you did today, etc.

- Create contests: photo contests, commenting contests, liking contests. You want to create things that inspire them to share or participate.
- Offer an incentive: Winner gets print of the month, discount in your shop, one of 10 commenters will get a free print.
- Encourage fans to share pictures of their collections, favorite pictures of their animals.

- Create a schedule: What time of day, how many times a day, how many times per week you will post. And what type of content you will be posting.
- Create a day & time for what content is posted: New art on Fridays? Studio Sales on Sundays? Illustration of the day Tuesdays?

CREATE URGENCY

It's important to create an urgency and rarity for your work on a social network because everything is posted in real time, exposure on Facebook is short term and not every follower will see your posts.

- Create rarity with limited times or limited offers.
- Creating urgency will help increase the exposure of that particular post across other timelines. More likes, comments or shares equals, more exposure for that post.

ADVERTISE YOUR PAGE

Even with the smallest investment in advertising, you can increase your fan base as well as potential sales through the use of Facebook ads. Facebook offers a user-friendly system that makes it simple for even the beginner. Perhaps you only advertise for a week around a special event or artwork you are working on.

PROMOTING A POST

Promoting a post increases the chances of that post being seen by your fans for a longer period of time. People log on at different times, for different lengths. Not everyone goes directly to the page to read what's happening. At any time you wish to cancel or pause a promotion, you can.

START NOW & GROW

- Post regularly – almost every day.
- Offer art weekly, through studio sales, special limited edition and print sales.
- Promote your other online sites.
- Revisit old events, old artworks and past experiences for content.
- Syndicate your blog and social networks to the page to increase content, social engagement and artwork awareness.

You could also use a similar technique to grow your Pinterest, Tumblr, twitter and Instagram account. Look at other social media sites and really widen your audience.

8 Tips For Selling Art On YouTube

8 TIPS FOR SELLING ART ON YOUTUBE

1. **Make a video that's fun to watch.** Your art is your passion, so let it shine through!

2. **Make it easy to find your videos.** YouTube is a giant search engine, more than 25% of all searches on the web happen on YouTube. Search Engine Optimization rules apply. Pay attention to your video title and description, links and tags

3. **Put your art on your channel as a background image.** By clicking on the Edit my Channel link, you can upload images as backgrounds.

4. **Calls to Action in your video**. What is the one thing that you want people to do after watching your video? Join your mailing list? Bid on an auction for your art? YouTube has an

editor that allows you to add little notes in the video, as well as clickable links. If you're showing multiple pieces of art in a single video, you could add links to each piece on your website.

5. **Post a bulletin.** People can subscribe to your YouTube channel. Be sure to post the occasional update and let them know what kind of interesting things you are currently doing.

6. **YouTube ads.** They are a great way to raise awareness about your work!

7. **Leverage your friends**. Facebook, Twitter, StumbleUpon and other sites are great ways to share your videos. Leverage your friends' networks by asking them to share your videos.

8. **YouTube analytics**. The information will tell you which of your videos are the most popular, where traffic is coming from, and which ones received the most activity.

Blogging to Sell Artwork

If you have a passion for your art, and you are longing to share that with the world. Then follow these five simple guidelines for starting your own blog, and you will catapult your artwork sells to a new high.

1. **Choose a host.** The first step to starting your blog is to pick a host. A "host" is a company that houses your blog online and allows it to be seen by your readers. If you choose a website that is centered around blogging then you are done with this step. If not, there are many great companies out there, but a WordPress site is one of the best.

2. **Choose a topic.** Chances are since you are a passionate artist, you already have a topic in mind.

3. **Be authentic.** You have a unique story and perspective. If you are willing to authentically share that on your blog, you won't have any trouble finding a group of readers and future buyers.

4. **Choose a domain name (aka website address).** A domain name is the web address people will type in to get to your blog. If you already have a website and web address, then there is no need to create another.

5. **Start an email List.** Collecting the email addresses of your loyal readers is one of the most important steps to growing your traffic and your blogging income. There are many email management companies, but MailChimp is a great start.

In addition to your artwork sales, you can earn additional money on ads, affiliate networks, sponsored posts, writing books, private or group video classes and much more.

Online Market Place Options

Selling online at one of these market places is a great way to increase sales, drive current and future buyers to your website, and have the ability to offer artwork to the entire world. However, with any 3ʳᵈ party selling options you will be paying a commission. This of course isn't the end of the world. For many of you who are not selling much on your own, paying the commissions and have a steady stream of income while increasing reputation, is worth every penny.

- AMAZON

  The biggest player in the U.S. online marketplace is Amazon. The site offers millions of different products to a huge diverse audience.

- EBAY

  You can find anything from electronics to fine art. As a seller, you can ask shoppers to bid on an item or buy it upfront.

- ETSY

  Etsy is similar to eBay, but is focused mostly handmade or vintage products.

- SHOPIFY

Simple and easy to set up, Shopify lets you build your own eCommerce store from scratch. It has a great interface, over a hundred mobile responsive themes and loads of amazing add-on apps.

- ZIBBET

If you're selling handmade goods this is a great place to check out.

- LEMONSTAND

LemonStand is all about growth, so if you have a new idea and want to develop it, this is an excellent option.

- ALIBABA

This Chinese company makes Amazon look small. Alibaba operates many online marketplaces, the largest being Alibaba and Taobao. The company is in the early stages of expanding into the U.S.

- JET

Jet is aiming at providing a low-cost marketplace using optimized shipping costs and a membership model similar to Costco. The service will carry branded products only, but for certain sellers it can be a great platform to reach consumers.

- BONANZA

Another great alternative to the big marketplaces. The site carries a wide variety of products, from fashion and jewelry to art and home furnishings, and offers sellers the ability to market their products via Google Shopping for a slightly higher fee.

- DEPOP

If you're looking for a mobile-optimized marketplace, this is a great place to start. All you have to do is use the app to take a photo and share your link on whatever platforms you want. They handle the sale itself and takes a small cut.

- VIDE DRESSING

If you're selling high-end fashion, Vide Dressing is a great site for your products, and the site makes things easy for low-volume sellers.

- MOVE LOOT

If you have furniture to sell online, Move Loot is the place to go. Submit your items via the website, and the company will pick it up and sell the items for you. It's a low-key, simple way to get rid of extra household items, and since the company lists the products for you, the process is as easy as it gets. Move Loot is only available in a few U.S. cities at the moment.

- FLIPKART

Flipkart is India's leading marketplace. If reaching rapidly developing markets is something that you're interested in, then check it out.

- ECRATER

eCRATER offers a different take on the eCommerce marketplace. It's a company that both helps you build a free online store and curates an online marketplace of millions of products on Google Shopping.

- CRAIGSLIST

Not exactly an eCommerce platform, but you can sell on Craigslist locally.

- CUSTOMMADE

If you create high-end custom products like jewelry or woodworking, they are worth at least checking them out.

Chapter 15: Lesser Know Places to Sell Art

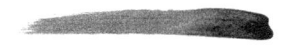

There are lesser known places to sell your art, which are especially useful when you are just starting out. Even though most people don't visit types venues to see or buy art, the show is still a line on your resume and you can still post images online.

Whether you end up selling or not, these types of venues are always good for improving your name recognition, so never pass up an opportunity to show at one, especially if you're early in your career or not currently represented by a gallery.

CONSIDER SHOWING AT PLACES LIKE:

- Restaurants
- Coffee shops
- Salons
- Clothing boutiques
- Bookstores
- Hotels
- Bed and breakfasts
- Designer furniture showrooms

As long as you can make your art look good, and you trust the place showing it, go ahead. Do your best to present your work in ways that visitors will have no doubt about it being worthy of attention, and have no doubt that every single piece of it is available for sale.

ADDITION EXPOSURE:

- Donating your art to select non-profit or charity auctions.
- Doing volunteer work for non-profit art organizations.
- Interning at galleries.
- Lending your art to businesses or organizations.
- Allow images of your art to appear on websites as illustrations, backgrounds or images.

Chapter 16: Turning Art into Unique Products

Get paid for putting your digital artwork images on products is not a bad gig. By stamping your artwork on everything from mouse pads, clothing, phone covers, posters, coffee mugs to holiday cards, you will be getting paid to strengthen your own artistic reputation.

There are a few market places that handle the entire process from print to ship, I would suggest doing some research to find the best match.

❖ Zazzle.com is one worth checking out. They only require you to upload your designs on any of their products, and they do everything else from printing, shipping to handling customer service.

Chapter 17: Licensing

Licensing your art is granting limited rights to a manufacturer, so they can display it on their products. They will pay a royalty in return for those rights.

It is a great way to place your art on a variety of products without having to manufacture, sell or warehouse the products.

HOW DO YOU GET INTO THE WORLD OF LICENSING?

- Create a strong body of work with many images, having a distinct style that's recognizable.
- Educate yourself on how licensing works. Get familiar with the contractual language and the general way the deals are made.
- Always retain ownership to the copyrights of your artwork.
- GET PREPARED to Present: You will need 10-12 images of a similar theme to approach a potential licensee. Don't ever go to a potential licensee and show them just 2 or 3 images, you'll lose credibility fast.

- Attend Licensing International in Las Vegas, NV in June. Walk the show, see what's going on, and attend the seminars.
- Take online classes on licensing or seek a licensing expert for advice.
- Find companies that you want to license with, sell the idea that your art will make them greater revenues.

Chapter 18: Copyright & Protect Your Art

Few artists are really at risk, especially those who produce more abstract or conceptual pieces. Those images that are easy to copy, particularly onto mediums such as T-shirts, coffee mugs, shoes, bags, skateboards, or similar types of merchandise are at higher risk. Also, artwork with creatures, characters or settings that could be replicated in films, animation, comics or video games. If you make art with any of these characteristics, registering the copyrights is highly recommended.

Copyrighting is also great if you have developed a look, composition or subject matter, that is identified as being uniquely yours. This is even more so if it's becoming increasingly popular with collectors.

BASICS OF LICENSING INFRINGEMENT

- Suppose that someone has reproduced some major characteristic of your art without your permission. If you have not registered that art prior to the infringement, you are limited to the infringer's profits as your damages.

- If the art is registered prior to the infringement, then in addition to statutory damages, the court can also award your attorney's fees plus other incidental costs of litigation.
- If your art is infringed on and it's not registered, you have to go ahead and register it anyways before you can bring a copyright action in federal court. Therefore, you are not saving anything by not registering it in advance.
- Registering your art in advance of an infringement proves that you created the image when you say you did.

For these reasons, attorneys are far more likely to take infringement cases on a contingency fee basis where the art has been registered prior to the infringements. Resolving claims on registered works of art is always easier for the attorneys and copyright holders since it predates the infringement.

Chapter 19: Pricing Art Right

1. Document the actual cost of materials and time. You need to stay profitable if you want to keep your hobby or business afloat. In addition, you need to be fair with your potential buyers and offer a piece that is worth the money. That may change over time, since your art is like real estate, the more demand the higher you can charge and still be fair.

2. Start lower. It's easier to start low and raise your prices than it is to lower your prices later.

3. Never ever undersell your galleries. You have one price for your art whether it's with a gallery, your studio or website.

4. Any gallery that gets wind that you sold at a lower price will drop you. When the word reaches other galleries, and it will, you will be told to take a hike.

5. If you don't have a gallery and don't want a gallery, you have more pricing freedom than other artists.

6. If you can't keep work in inventory, because they sell too fast, it's probably time to raise your prices.

7. Larger works are usually more expensive than smaller works.
8. Works made from higher-priced materials have a bigger price tag.
9. Works on canvas often command more than works on paper. But then there's that whole framing thing. You must frame works on paper to demand better prices.
10. Likewise, bronze sculptures have higher prices than carved wood.
11. Conduct market research to find comparable work. Look for artists who do similar work, using similar materials, and who are at a similar place in their career.
12. Keep a price list. When someone asks you how much something is, you want to be able to tell them quickly and effortlessly.
13. Radiate confidence. It's remarkable how powerful this trick is. Spend time deciding on the prices, then have confidence in them.

Chapter 20: Final Thoughts

There are as many ways to sell art, and become successful as there are artists. Each and every one of those ways is OK. Never forget that exceptional art is based on the expression of your unique inner-self. The same is true for the journey you will take to reach your goals and aspirations as an artist.

www.ingramcontent.com/pod-product-compliance
Lightning Source LLC
Chambersburg PA
CBHW071229220526
45468CB00002B/778